The Boy Who Cried Wolf

Based on a traditional tale
Robyn Green and Bronwen Scarffe

Illustrated by
Sue O'Loughlin

The Boy Who Cried Wolf

Primary Education

LONG, long ago, there lived a shepherd boy. Each day he kept watch over the village sheep high in the hills.

He often passed the time by telling stories and singing songs to the sheep but they took no notice. They just continued to chew the sweet grass, bleating softly to one another.

WOLF! WOLF!

SOME days the shepherd boy enjoyed himself and the time passed quickly. Other days were long and lonely.

It was on one such day when the shepherd boy was feeling bored and restless, that he cried out to the village below, 'Wolf! Wolf!'.

WOLF! WOLF!

8

THE villagers came panting up the steep hillside to drive the wolf away. But all they found were the sheep grazing peacefully and the shepherd boy laughing. There was no wolf in sight.

They returned to their homes annoyed with the shepherd boy for wasting their time.

WOLF! WOLF! A WOLF IS HERE!

T was on another such day when the shepherd boy was feeling even more bored and restless that he cried out again to the village below, 'Wolf! Wolf! A wolf is here'.

Once again the villagers came panting up the steep hillside to drive the wolf away. But all they found were the sheep grazing peacefully and the shepherd boy laughing. Again there was no wolf in sight.

NCE more they returned to the village annoyed with the shepherd boy for wasting their time and playing such a stupid trick.

Alas, one winter's afternoon a wolf really did set upon the sheep. The shepherd boy cried out in earnest, 'Help! Help! The wolf is here and it is taking the sheep!'.

WOLF! HELP!

WOLF! WOLF!

14

THIS time the villagers didn't come panting up the steep hillside to drive the wolf away. They ignored the shepherd boy's call for help, and the wolf devoured the sheep.

MORAL

No-one believes a liar –

even when they tell the truth.